Air Fryer Toaster Oven Recipes

Crispy, Easy and Delicious Recipes that Anyone Can Cook and Want to Enjoy Tasty Effortless Dishes

Table of Contents

INTRODUCTION: 8

CHAPTER 1: UNTOLD BENEFITS OF AN AIR FRYER YOU MAY NOT KNOW 10

CHAPTER 2: AIR FRYER OVEN TIPS & TRICKS AND ITS FUNCTION KEYS 12

    CHECK FOOD DURING COOKING 13

    CLEANING THE AIR FRYER 13

    FUNCTION KEYS 13

CHAPTER 3: BREAKFAST 16

    1. AIR FRYER BAKED EGG CUPS WITH SPINACH & CHEESE 16

    2. BREAKFAST CASSEROLE 18

    3. CHEESY BACON AND EGG HASH 20

    4. BACON CHEDDAR BISCUITS 22

    5. POTATO HASH BROWN CASSEROLE 24

    6. SWEET POTATO CASSEROLE 26

CHAPTER 4: MAINS 28

    7. BASIL CHICKEN BITES 28

    8. PAPRIKA COD 30

    9. TURKEY AND MUSHROOM STEW 31

CHAPTER 5: SIDES 32

    10. BALSAMIC CABBAGE 32

    11. HERBED RADISH SAUTÉ 34

    12. ROASTED TOMATOES 35

CHAPTER 6: SEAFOOD 38

    13. COD AND TOMATOES 38

    14. SPICY TILAPIA 39

15. Garlic Lime Shrimp 41

16. Dijon Salmon 42

17. Tasty Shrimp Fajitas 43

18. Parmesan Walnut Salmon 44

CHAPTER 7: POULTRY **46**

19. Mustard Turkey Bites 46

20. Turkey Turnovers 48

21. Chicken Pram 50

22. Teriyaki Duck Legs 52

23. Crunchy Almond & Kale Salad With Roasted Chicken 54

CHAPTER 8: MEAT **56**

24. Lamb Rack With Lemon Crust 56

25. Braised Lamb Shanks 58

26. Za'atar Lamb Chops 60

27. Simple Beef Sirloin Roast 62

28. Seasoned Beef Roast 64

29. Bacon-Wrapped Filet Mignon 66

30. Beef Burgers 68

CHAPTER 9: VEGETABLES **70**

31. Blistered Shishito Peppers 70

32. Mascarpone Mushrooms 72

33. Air Fried Asparagus 74

34. Cheesy Macaroni Balls 75

35. Crispy Chickpeas 77

CHAPTER 10: SOUP **78**

36. Broccoli And Chicken Soup 78

CHAPTER 11: SNACKS **80**

37.   POTATO NUGGETS...80

38.   TASTY ZUCCHINI PATTIES 82

39.   BEEF ENCHILADA DIP 84

40.   MEATBALLS IN THERMO MIX AND AIR FRYER 86

41.   FRIED SARDINES IN THE AIR FRYER 88

CHAPTER 12: DESSERTS **90**

42.   CHERRY PANCAKES 90

43.   APPLE FRITTERS 92

44.   PEANUT BUTTER BANANA BITES..94

45.   HEALTHY APPLE CRISP 95

46.   CRANBERRY SCONES 97

47.   BLUEBERRY APPLE CRUMBLE 99

48.   AIR FRIED APPLE PIE 101

49.   AIR FRYER BISCUIT DONUTS 103

CHAPTER 13: SPECIAL RECIPE **104**

50.   SWEET BABY CARROTS DISH 104

CONCLUSION **106**

Introduction:

A Low-Fat Meals: Unarguably, the most fundamental advantage of the air fryer is its use of hot-air course to cook food ingredients from all points, accordingly taking out the need for oil use. That makes it workable for people on a low-fat eating regimen to serenely get ready for magnificently good meals. More beneficial Foods& Environment: Air fryers are intended to work without stuffing oils and deliver more good foods with up to 80 percent less fat. That makes it simpler to shed pounds because you can eat your seared dishes while saving calories and immersed fat. Making that change to a more useful life is progressively feasible by utilizing this appliance. Your house is also freed of the fragrance that accompanies deep singed foods that regularly remain around the climate even a few hours after deep searing.

Multipurpose Use: The air fryer empowers you to perform various tasks to set up numerous dishes immediately. You're across the board appliance that can flame broil, bake, fry, and meal those dishes you love! You never again need numerous machines for different occupations. It can do other employments separate appliances will do. It can flame broil meat, cook veggies, and bake baked goods. It fills in as a compelling substitution for your broiler, deep fryer, and stovetop.

Very Safe: Remember how extra cautious you must be while tossing chicken or some different ingredients into the deep fryer? You need to guarantee that the hot oil doesn't spill and consume your skin since it's in every case hot. With your air-fryer, you wouldn't need to stress over brunt skin from hot oil spillage. It does all the broiling and is protected. By and by, use cooking gloves while repositioning your fryer to maintain a strategic distance from risks from the warmth. Moreover, keep your air fryer out of kids' span.

Simple Clean Up: The Air Fryer leaves no oil and, consequently, no wreckage. Clean-up time is pleasant since their oils spill to clean on dividers and floors, and no rejecting or scouring of the skillet. There is no need to invest in energy, guaranteeing that everything is immaculate. The Air fryer parts are made of a non-stick material that keeps food from adhering to surfaces, making it difficult to clean. These parts are anything but difficult to clean and keep up. They are removable and dishwasher-protected also.

Spare Valuable Time: People on tight timetables can utilize the air fryer's quickness to make delightful meals. For cases, you can make French fries in less than 15 minutes and bake a cake inside 25 minutes. Inside minutes as well, you can appreciate firm chicken fingers or brilliant fries. If you are consistently in a hurry, the air fryer is perfect for you because you will invest less energy in the kitchen. It empowers you to deal with your boisterous and occupied day by day life, making your day progressively sensible.

CHAPTER 1:

Untold Benefits of an Air Fryer You May Not Know

You may begin to wonder why you need to use an air fryer and those things that make it unique. Well, you are not alone on this. Many people have been in your shoes before as they wondered why the hype about air fryers. I used to think like that too, but now I know better! An air fryer has many untold benefits, and here are some of them.

Health wise, an air fryer is great because it helps you healthily prepare food. If you recall, too much oil is not suitable for your health, but when you deep-fry, you have no choice but to immerse the food in fat, and it absorbs most of the oil. That is why fried foods are not healthy because they soak up too much oil while in the preparation process. Unfortunately, you eventually consume this oil.

Apart from the health benefits of using an air fryer, other astonishing features make it stand out. One of them is that it is energy efficient and quick. For instance, for you to preheat your standard oven, it could take about fifteen (15) to twenty (20) minutes, but that's a different case when it comes to an air fryer.

With the unique design that makes an air fryer so compact, you don't have to wait for so long to preheat because it is cut down to just two (2) or three (3) minutes! With this, you don't just save time; you save energy too. You don't need to worry about heating the whole kitchen in summer because you can preheat your air fryer, and the entire kitchen won't be heated up.

Why should you spend so much time cooking when you can get things done faster with an air fryer? Due to the intense heat created when using an air fryer, meals are cooked pretty quickly than in an oven, about 20% faster, saving energy. You probably don't have much time to spare while cooking, and the manufacturers of your air fryer know about this, designing the cooking device in a way that will help you save time.

The air fryer is safer and easier to use than deep-frying because this cooking appliance mostly has settings for your preferred temperature and time. With the scenes, all you have to do set your preferences, and that's all! You don't have to go through the stress of heating a pot containing oil on your stovetop or register temperature with a deep-frying thermometer.

What about the stress of continually checking the heat below to ensure that the temperature is stable? The emphasis is just too much. Since you are dealing with lots of oil that can become a danger when very hot and getting rid of the fat can be tiring, why not save yourself from this stress by using an air fryer?

I know that feeling and how irritating it can be when your kitchen is messed up after cooking. Keeping the kitchen clean and tidy at all times is a must, and with an air fryer, you can achieve this quickly. Unlike your conventional cooking method, an air fryer prevents food from splattering around because everything you are cooking with is kept in a sealed space. Not just that, you can easily clean and maintain the air fryer, and I will share some helpful tips to do so.

CHAPTER 2:

Air Fryer Oven Tips & Tricks and Its Function Keys

A ir fryer Ovens are designed to be super easy to use. The air fryer does a great job of making food crispy because of the convection function. Here's a little tip to get you started:

Choosing a Recipe

Choose a recipe that you can cook in your air fryer. You can use my air fryer cookbook to help you find suitable recipes.

Preparing the Air Fryer

Read through the recipe to the end, so you know what accessories you need for cooking. Some recipes call for using the basket, rack, or rotisserie that comes with the air fryer. Other recipes use cake or muffin pans that you can insert into the air fryer. Just be sure these pans fit into the fryer and are safe to use.

Preparing the Ingredients

Gather the ingredients for the recipe and prep them according to the instructions. When prepped, put the ingredients into the air fryer or in the basket, rack, or pans within the air fryer. Use parchment baking paper or a light mist of oil spray to prevent food from sticking.

Never crowd food in the air fryer or over-fill. Food that is sealed in the air fryer won't cook evenly and can be raw and under-cooked. If you're preparing for a crowd, you may have to cook more than one batch.

Setting the Temperature and Time

Check the recipe for the correct temperature and time setting. You can set manually; you can use the digital location for the weather and time needed for the recipe. Most air fryers also have preset functions that make it easy to set according to each recipe.

Check Food During Cooking

Many air fryer oven recipes require you to check the food while cooking to cooks evenly and don't over-cook. You will need to shake, flip, or toss the food to distribute it. Or for some recipes, you'll need to turn the food about halfway through when cooking so that it cooks and crisps all the way thoroughly.

Cleaning The Air Fryer

Some air fryers use a round basket where foods are cooked, while other models will have layered racks that fit into a square cooking space, much like a small oven. Most of the recipes given in this cookbook can be used for both baskets and racks.

Keep an Eye on Timing

You'll find that air fryers cook at different temperatures depending on what model you have. It's essential to check on foods during the cooking process, so you don't over or undercook them. If you've cut back on quantities in some of the recipes, be sure to cut the cooking time down accordingly.

Remember, hints are just recommendations to guide you as you use your air fryer.

Using Oil Sprays

Most of the recipes use an oil spray. But if you desire, you can use any brand you want. Or make your own by merely putting olive oil into a small spray bottle. Use a small amount of fat and spray over the basket and trays to prevent food from sticking. Some of the recipes require you to stream the food with oil directly.

Function Keys

The following are the functions keys of an Air Fryer Oven:

Play/Pause Button

This Play/Pause button allows you to pause during the middle of the cooking so you can shake the air fryer basket or flip the food to ensure it cooks evenly.

-/+ Button /Minus or Plus Button

This button is used to change the time or temperature.

Keep Warm

This function keeps your food warm for 30 minutes.

Food Presets

This button gives you the ability to cook food without second-guessing. The time and temperature are already set, so new users find this setting useful.

Roast or Broil

You can roast or broil with this setting. When using a conventional oven, you need to brown the meat before roasting. You can skip this step when cooking with an air fryer.

CHAPTER 3:

BREAKFAST

1.   Air Fryer Baked Egg Cups With Spinach & Cheese

Preparation Time: 10 minutes

Cooking Time: 30minutes

Serving: 4

Ingredients

- Milk 1 tablespoon

- Cheese 1-2 teaspoons

- Egg 1 large

- Frozen spinach one tablespoon

- Cooking spray

- Salt and black pepper

Directions:

1.   Spray with oil spray inside the silicone muffin cups.

2. In a muffin cup, incorporate the cream, potato, spinach, and cheese.

3. Gently combine the egg whites with the liquids without separating the yolk and salt and pepper to taste.

4. For around 6-12 minutes, Air Fried at 330 ° F (single egg cups typically take about five minutes-several or doubled cups require as many as 12.

5. It may take a bit longer to cook in a ceramic ramekin. Cook for less time if you like runny yolks. After 5 minutes, regularly check the eggs to make sure the egg is of your desired texture.

2.   Breakfast Casserole

Preparation Time: 10 minutes

Cooking Time: 55 minutes

Serving: 8

Ingredients:

- 1 lb. bacon, chopped

- One tablespoon olive oil

- Ten eggs

- ½ cup heavy cream

- 1 cup milk

- One teaspoon garlic powder

- One onion, diced

- 2 Roma tomatoes, seeded and chopped

- One green bell pepper, seeded and chopped

- 1 cup white cheddar, shredded

- ½ cup mozzarella cheese, shredded

- 28 oz. hash browns, frozen and shredded

- Salt and black pepper, to taste

Directions:

1. Grease a baking tray with cooking spray.

2. Heat oil in a skillet over medium heat. Add bacon and cook for 8 minutes. Add onion and cook for 3 minutes.

3. Whisk milk, eggs, cream, and garlic powder in a bowl—season with salt and pepper. Add onion, bell pepper, tomatoes, bacon, and cheddar cheese.

4. Add a layer of hash browns to the bottom of the tray. Add the egg mixture over the hash browns. Top with mozzarella.

5. Position the baking tray in Rack Position 2 and select the Bake setting. Set the temperature to 350 F and the time to 50 minutes. Serve.

Nutrition:

548 calories; 42 g fat; 18 g total carbs; 23 g protein

3. Cheesy Bacon And Egg Hash

Preparation Time: 10 minutes

Cooking Time: 35 minutes

Serving: 4

Ingredients:

- 7 oz. diced bacon, trimmed fat

- 24 oz. potatoes, scrubbed and peeled

- Two tablespoons olive oil

- Two scallions, trimmed and sliced

- ¼ cup Mozzarella cheese, shredded

- Four eggs

- Salt, pepper, to taste

Directions:

1. Cut potatoes into small cubes.

2. Arrange the potatoes in a single layer on a baking pan. Grease with cooking spray and position the baking pan in Rack Position 2.

3. Select the Bake setting. Set the temperature to 30 and the time to 400F. Stir once halfway.

4. Remove from the oven, add bacon, and bake for 10 minutes.

5. Make four wells in the hash and add an egg into each well. Add mozzarella around each egg. Add the pan back to the oven and bake until eggs are done. Serve.

Nutrition:

413 calories; 28 g fat; 18 g total carbs; 17 g protein

4. Bacon Cheddar Biscuits

Preparation Time: 10 minutes Cooking Time: 95 minutes

Serving: 8

Ingredients:

- One tablespoon baking powder

- Four slices of bacon

- 3 ½ cup all-purpose flour

- ½ teaspoon baking soda

- Two teaspoons granulated sugar

- ½ cup cheddar cheese, shredded

- One ¼ cup buttermilk, chilled

- ¼ cup green onions, sliced

- 1 cup + 2 tablespoons unsalted butter

- Two teaspoons kosher salt

Directions:

1. Add bacon to a baking pan. Position the baking pan in Rack Position 2 and select the Bake setting. Set the temperature to 375 F and the time to 20 minutes. Drain on paper towels and chop once cool.

2. Whisk baking powder, flour, baking soda, sugar, and salt in a bowl. Cut 1 cup cold butter into 1/8" pieces. Add few butter slices into flour and stir well to break the butter pieces. Freeze the mixture for 15 minutes.

3. Add cheddar cheese, bacon, and green onions to flour mixture. Stir well.

4. Add one ¼ cups buttermilk into the flour mixture and stir well. Knead the biscuit mixture a few times.

5. Dust a surface with flour and divide the dough into two parts.

6. Roll out the dough into a 1" thick square. Cut dough into four even-shaped squares and stack on top of each other. Leave ¼" border along the edges. Use a biscuit cutter to form cookies.

7. Add to a baking pan and repeat with the remaining dough. Refrigerate for 30 minutes before baking.

8. Melt two tablespoons of butter and brush on top of each biscuit. Sprinkle with salt.

9. Position the baking pan in Rack Position 2 and select the Bake setting. Set the temperature to 450 F and the time to 15 minutes. Cool for 10 minutes. Serve.

Nutrition:

410 calories; 21.4 g fat; 44 g total carbs; 9 g protein

5. Potato Hash Brown Casserole

Preparation Time: 15 minutes Cooking Time: 75 minutes

Serving: 12

Ingredients:

- 1 lb. sausages, casings removed
- One large sweet potato, peeled and diced into ½" chunks
- One red onion, chopped
- Two bell peppers, deseeded and diced
- One teaspoon garlic, minced
- 2 cups baby spinach leaves, washed
- 1 cup mushrooms, sliced
- 1 cup grape tomatoes, halved
- Ten eggs
- 1/3 cup milk
- 2/3 cup mozzarella cheese, shredded
- Salt and black pepper, to taste

Directions:

1. Grease a casserole dish with cooking spray.

2.   Heat 1 tablespoon oil in a skillet over medium heat. Add sweet potatoes and fry for 2 minutes, stirring. Cover with lid and cook for 10 minutes, stirring occasionally. Transfer to the casserole dish.

3.   Fry sausage meat in the skillet and break it up. Cook until done. Add garlic and onion and fry until onion is transparent. Add mushrooms and peppers and cook for 3 minutes, stirring occasionally.

4.   Add spinach and cook until it wilts. Season well. Transfer veggies and sausages to the dish. Add sliced tomatoes and mix all ingredients.

5.   Whisk eggs in a bowl with 1/3 cup cheese and milk.

6.   Add the eggs over the casserole dish. Add remaining 1/3 cup cheese. Season well.

7.   Position the oven to reach in Rack Position 1 and place the dish on top. Select the Bake setting. Set the temperature to 375 F and the time to 45 minutes.

8.   Cool slightly. Slice and serve.

Nutrition:

248 calories; 15.2 g fat; 12 g total carbs; 18 g protein

6.   Sweet Potato Casserole

Preparation Time: 10 minutes

Cooking Time: 35 minutes

Serving: 8

Ingredients:

- ½ cup granulated sugar

- 4 cups sweet potatoes, cooked and peeled

- ¼ cup unsalted butter

- ¼ cup milk

- Two teaspoons pure vanilla extract

- Two large eggs whisked

- ½ teaspoon salt

- ½ cup light brown sugar

- ½ cup all-purpose flour

- Two tablespoons unsalted butter

- ½ cup pecans, crushed

- Two tablespoons cinnamon sugar

- ½ teaspoon salt

Directions:

1. Grease a baking pan with cooking spray.

2. Mix sweet potatoes with milk, sugar, vanilla, ¼ cup butter, eggs, and ½ teaspoon salt in a bowl. Spread on a baking pan

3. Mix brown sugar, flour, butter, pecans, and salt in a separate bowl. Mix well. Add evenly over the sweet potatoes. Top with cinnamon sugar.

4. Position the baking pan in Rack Position 2 and select the Bake setting. Set the temperature to 350 F and the time to 25 minutes.

5. Select the Broil setting. Set the temperature to Broil and the time to 10. Serve.

Nutrition: 225 calories; 11 g fat; 34 g total carbs; 4 g protein

CHAPTER 4:

Mains

7.   Basil Chicken Bites

Preparation Time: 10 minutes

Cooking Time: 30 minutes

Serving: 4

Ingredients:

- 1 ½ lb. chicken breasts, skinless; boneless and cubed

- ½ cup chicken stock

- ½ tsp. basil; dried

- 2 tsp. smoked paprika

- Salt and black pepper to taste.

Directions:

1. In a pan that fits the air fryer, combine all the ingredients, toss, introduce the pan in the fryer and cook at 390°F for 25 minutes

2. Divide between plates and serve for lunch with a side salad.

Nutrition: Calories: 223; Fat: 12g; Fiber: 2g; Carbs: 5g; Protein: 13g

8.   Paprika Cod

Preparation Time: 10 minutes Cooking Time: 17 minutes

Serving: 4

Ingredients:

- 1 lb. cod fillets, boneless, skinless, and cubed

- One spring onion; chopped.

- 2 cups baby arugula

- 2 tbsp. Fresh cilantro; minced

- ½ tsp. Sweet paprika

- ½ tsp. oregano, ground

- A drizzle of olive oil

- Salt and black pepper to taste.

Directions:

1. Take a bowl and mix the cod with salt, pepper, paprika, oregano, and the oil, toss, transfer the cubes to your air fryer's basket and cook at 360°F for 12 minutes

2. In a salad bowl, mix the cod with the remaining ingredients, toss, divide between plates and serve.

Nutrition: Calories: 240; Fat: 11g; Fiber: 3g; Carbs: 5g; Protein: 8g

9.   Turkey And Mushroom Stew

Preparation Time: 10 minutes

Cooking Time: 30 minutes

Serving: 4

Ingredients:

- ½ lb. brown mushrooms; sliced

- One turkey breast, skinless, boneless; cubed and browned

- ¼ cup tomato sauce

- 1 tbsp. Parsley, chopped.

- Salt and black pepper

Directions:

1.   In a pan that fits your air fryer, mix the turkey with the mushrooms, salt, pepper, and tomato sauce toss, introduce to the fryer and cook at 350°F for 25 minutes

2.   Divide into bowls and serve for lunch with parsley sprinkled on top.

Nutrition: Calories: 220; Fat: 12g; Fiber: 2g; Carbs: 5g; Protein: 12g

CHAPTER 5:

Sides

10.   Balsamic Cabbage

Preparation Time: 10 minutes

Cooking Time: 15 minutes

Servings: 4

Ingredients:

- 6 cups red cabbage; shredded

- Four garlic cloves; minced

- 1 tbsp. olive oil

- 1 tbsp. balsamic vinegar

- Salt and black pepper

Directions:

1.   In a frying pan that fits the deep fryer, combine all ingredients, mix, place skillet in the deep fryer, and cook at

380 ° F for 15 minutes. Divide between dishes and serve as a garnish.

Nutrition:

Calories: 151

Fat 2g

Carbs: 5g

Protein 5g

11.　Herbed Radish Sauté

Preparation Time: 5 minutes

Cooking Time: 15 minutes

Servings: 4

Ingredients:

- Two bunches red radishes; halved
- 2 tbsp. Parsley, chopped.
- 2 tbsp. balsamic vinegar
- 1 tbsp. olive oil
- Salt and black pepper

Directions:

1. Take a bowl and mix the radishes with the remaining ingredients except for the parsley, toss and put them in your air fryer's basket.

2. Cook at 400°F for 15 minutes, divide between plates, sprinkle the parsley on top and serve as a side dish

Nutrition:

Calories: 180 Fat 4g

Carbs: 3g

Protein 5g

12.   Roasted Tomatoes

Preparation Time: 5 minutes

Cooking Time: 15 minutes

Servings: 4

Ingredients:

- Four tomatoes; halved
- ½ cup parmesan; grated
- 1 tbsp. basil; chopped.
- ½ tsp. Onion powder
- ½ tsp. Oregano; dried
- ½ tsp. Smoked paprika
- ½ tsp. garlic powder
- Cooking spray

Directions:

1. Get a bowl and add up all the ingredients except the cooking spray and the parmesan.

2. Arrange the tomatoes in your air fryer's pan, sprinkle the parmesan on top, and grease with cooking spray

3.   Cook at 370°F for 15 minutes, divide between plates, and serve.

Nutrition:

Calories: 200

Fat 7g

Carbs: 4g

Protein 6g

CHAPTER 6:

Seafood

13.   Cod And Tomatoes

Preparation 20 minutes Cooking 15 minutesServings: 4

Ingredients:

- 1 cup cherry tomatoes; halved

- Four cod fillets, skinless and boneless

- 2 tbsp. olive oil

- 2 tbsp. Cilantro; chopped.

- Salt and black pepper

Directions:

1. In a baking dish that fits your air fryer, mix all the ingredients, and toss gently.

2. Introduce in your air fryer and cook at 370°F for 15 minutes

3. Divide everything between plates and serve right away.

Nutrition: Calories: 248; Fat: 11g; Fiber: 2g; Carbs: 5g; Protein: 11g

14.   Spicy Tilapia

Preparation Time: 20 minutes

Cooking Time: 25 minutes

Servings: 4

Ingredients:

- 4 tilapia fillets

- 1/2 tsp. red chili powder

- 1 tsp. garlic, minced

- 3 tbsp. butter, melted

- 1 tbsp. fresh lemon juice

- 2 tsps. fresh parsley, chopped

- 1 lemon, sliced

- Pepper

- Salt

Directions:

1.   Line the Baking Pan with foil and set aside.

2.   Place fish fillets in the baking pan and season with pepper and salt.

3.   Mix together butter, red chili powder, garlic, and lemon juice and pour over fish fillets.

4.   Arrange lemon slices on top of fish fillets.

5.   Place the baking pan into rack position 2.

6.   Set to Convection Bake at 350°F for 15 minutes.

7.   Garnish with parsley and serve.

Nutrition:

Calories 149

Fat 12 g

Carbohydrates 4 g

Sugar 0.1 g

Protein 6 g

Cholesterol 38 mg

15.   Garlic Lime Shrimp

Preparation 20 minutes Cooking 20 minutes Servings: 4

Ingredients:

- 1 lb. shrimp, peel and deveined

- 2 tbsps. lime juice

- 2 tbsps. butter, melted

- 1/4 cup fresh cilantro, chopped

- 3 garlic cloves, pressed

Directions:

1. Line the Baking Pan with foil and set aside.

2. Add shrimp into the baking dish.

3. Mix together garlic, lime juice, and butter and pour over shrimp.

4. Toss shrimp well and let it sit for 15 minutes.

5. Place the baking pan into rack position 2.

6. Set to Convection Bake at 375°F for 15 minutes.

7. Garnish with cilantro and serve.

Nutrition: Calories 195 Fat 7.7 g Carbohydrates 4.4 g Sugar 0.4 g

Protein 26.1 g Cholesterol 254 mg

16. Dijon Salmon

Preparation Time: 20 minutes Cooking Time: 22minutes

Servings: 4 Ingredients:

- 4 salmon fillets
- 1/4 cup Dijon mustard
- 1/4 cup maple syrup
- 2garlic cloves, minced
- 2 tbsp olive oil
- Pepper
- Salt

Directions:

1. Line the Baking Pan with foil and set aside.
2. Place salmon fillets into the baking pan.
3. Mix garlic, olive oil, Dijon mustard, maple syrup, pepper, salt, and pour over salmon. Coat well and let sit for 10 minutes.
4. Place the baking pan into rack position 2.
5. Set to Convection Bake at 400°F for 12 minutes.

Nutrition: Calories 360 Fat 18 g Carbohydrates 14 g Sugar 12 g

Protein 35 g Cholesterol 78 mg

17.   Tasty Shrimp Fajitas

Preparation Time: 10 minutes

Cooking Time: 25 minutes

Servings: 4

Ingredients:

- lb. shrimp, peeled and deveined

- 1bell peppers, sliced

- 1 medium onion, sliced

- 1/2 lime juice

- 1 1/2 tbsp. taco seasoning

- 1 1/2 tbsp. olive oil

Directions:

1.   Line the Baking Pan with foil and set aside.

2.   In a bowl, toss shrimp with remaining ingredients.

3.   Spread shrimp mixture on a baking pan.

4.   Place the baking pan into rack position 2.

5.   Set to Convection Bake at 400°F for 15 minutes.

Nutrition: Calories 229 Fat 8 g Carbohydrates 12 g Sugar 5 g Protein 27 g Cholesterol 240 mg

18. Parmesan Walnut Salmon

Preparation Time: 10 minutes

Cooking Time: 25 minutes

Servings: 4

Ingredients:

- 4 salmon fillets
- 1/4 cup walnuts
- 1 tsps. olive oil
- 1/4 cup parmesan cheese, grated
- 1 tbsp. lemon rind

Directions:

1. Line the Baking Pan with foil and set aside.

2. Place salmon fillets in the baking pan.

3. Add walnuts into the blender and blend until ground.

4. Mix together walnuts, cheese, oil, and lemon rind and spread on top of salmon fillets.

5. Place the baking pan into rack position 2.

6. Set to Convection Bake at 400°F for 15 minutes.

Nutrition: Calories 312 Fat 18 g Carbohydrates 1 g Sugar 0.2 g Protein 38 g Cholesterol 83 mg

CHAPTER 7:

Poultry

19.   Mustard Turkey Bites

Preparation Time: 5 minutes

Cooking Time: 20 minutes

Servings: 4

Ingredients:

- One big turkey breast, skinless; boneless, and cubed

- Four garlic cloves; minced

- 1 tbsp. mustard

- 1 ½ tbsp. olive oil

- Salt and black pepper to taste.

Directions:

1. Take a bowl and mix the chicken with the garlic and the other ingredients and toss.

2. Put the turkey in your air fryer's basket, cook at 360°F for 20 minutes, divide between plates and serve with a side salad

Nutrition:

Calories: 240 kcal/Cal

Fat: 12 g

Fiber: 4 g

Carbohydrates: 6 g

Protein: 15g

20.   Turkey Turnovers

Preparation Time: 10 minutes

Cooking time: 10 minutes

Servings: 8

Ingredients:

- 2 cups turkey, cooked & chopped

- 1 cup cheddar cheese, grated

- 1 cup broccoli, cooked & chopped

- ½ cup mayonnaise

- ½ tsp. salt

- ¼ tsp. pepper

- Two cans of refrigerated crescent rolls

Directions:

1. Place the baking pan in position 1 of the oven.

2. In a large bowl, combine all ingredients, except rolls, mix well.

3. Separate each can of rolls into four squares, press perforations to seal.

4. Spoon turkey mixture in the center of each square. Fold over diagonally and seal the edges.

5. Set oven to bake at 375°F for 15 minutes.

6. Brush tops of turnovers lightly with additional mayonnaise. After the oven has preheated for 5 minutes, place turnovers on baking pan and cook 10-12 minutes or until golden brown; serve warm.

Nutrition:

Calories: 309 kcal/Cal

Total Fat: 21 g

Saturated Fat: 6 g

Cholesterol: 0 mg

Sodium: 0 mg

Total Carbs: 15 g

Fiber: 2 g

Sugar: 1 g

Protein: 15 g

21. Chicken Pram

Preparation 10 minutes Cooking 35 minutes Servings: 4

Ingredients:

- Nonstick cooking spray

- ½ cup flour

- Two eggs

- 2/3 cup panko breadcrumbs

- 2/3 cup Italian seasoned breadcrumbs

- 1/3 + ¼ cup parmesan cheese, divided

- 2 tbsp. fresh parsley, chopped

- ½ tsp. salt

- ¼ tsp. pepper

- Four chicken breast halves, skinless & boneless

- 24 oz. marinara sauce

- 1 cup mozzarella cheese, grated

Directions:

1. Place the baking pan in position 2 of the oven. Lightly spray the fryer basket with cooking spray.

2. Place flour in a shallow dish.

3. In a separate shallow dish, beat the eggs.

4. In a third shallow dish, combine both breadcrumbs, 1/3 cup parmesan cheese, two tablespoons parsley, salt, and pepper.

5. Place chicken between two sheets of plastic wrap and pound to ½-inch thick.

6. Dip chicken first in flour, then eggs, and breadcrumb mixture to coat. Place in the basket and then put the basket on the baking pan.

7. Set oven to air fry on 375°F for 10 minutes. Turn chicken over halfway through cooking time.

8. Remove chicken and baking pan from the oven. Place the rack in position 1. Set range to bake on 425°F for 30 minutes.

9. Pour 1 ½ cups marinara in the bottom of an 8x11-inch baking dish. Place chicken over the sauce and add another two tablespoons marinara to tops of chicken. Top the chicken with mozzarella and parmesan cheese once oven preheats for 5 minutes, place the dish in the oven and bake 20-25 minutes until bubbly and cheese is golden brown. Serve.

Nutrition:

Calories: 529 kcal/Cal Total Fat: 13 g Saturated Fat: 5 g Cholesterol: 0 mg Sodium: 1437 mg otal Carbs: 52 g Fiber: 5 g

Sugar: 9 g Protein: 51 g

22.   Teriyaki Duck Legs

Preparation Time: 15 minutes

Cooking time: 2 hours

Servings: 6

Ingredients:

- 3 lbs. duck legs

- ½ cup teriyaki sauce

- 2 tbsp. soy sauce

- 2 tbsp. malt vinegar

Directions:

1. Place the rack in position 1 of the oven.

2. Place the duck legs, skin side up, in an 8x11-inch baking dish.

3. In a small bowl, whisk together the remaining ingredients and pour around duck legs. The liquid needs to reach the skin level. If not, add water until it does.

4. Set the oven to convection bake at 300°F for 60 minutes. After 5 minutes, place the ducks in the range and cook 90 minutes, or until tender.

5. Remove duck from the oven. Pour off cooking liquid into a small saucepan. Skim off fat and reserve. Bring sauce to a boil

and cook until it reduces, about 10 minutes, stirring occasionally.

6. Place the baking pan in position 2 of the oven. Place the duck legs in the fryer basket and brush with reserved fat and sauce. Place the basket in the oven and set to broil at 400°F for 10 minutes. Turn duck over halfway through and brush with fat and sauce again. Serve.

Nutrition:

Calories: 608 kcal/Cal

Total Fat: 20 g

Saturated Fat: 5 g

Cholesterol: 0 mg

Sodium: 1063 mg

Total Carbs: 6 g

Fiber: 0 g

Sugar: 5 g

Protein: 101 g

23.   Crunchy Almond & Kale Salad With Roasted Chicken

Preparation Time: 10 minutes

Cooking Time: 20 minutes

Servings: 1

Ingredients:

- Salad

- 1 teaspoon extra virgin olive oil

- 100g Lacinato kale, sliced into thin strips

- 1/4 cup roasted almonds

- Pinch of sea salt

- Pinch of pepper

- Roasted Chicken

- 100g chicken thighs

- Pinch of sea salt

- Pinch of pepper

- 1 teaspoon apple cider vinegar

- 1/2 teaspoon extra-virgin olive oil

- 1 tablespoon rosemary

- 1 tablespoon cup sage

Directions:

1.   Place kale in a bowl and add olive oil; massage olive oil with hands into the kale until kale is tender; sprinkle with salt and pepper and toss with toasted almonds.

2.   Preheat your air fryer toast oven to 360°F.

3.   Sprinkle chicken with salt and pepper; add vinegar and olive oil and season with rosemary and sage.

4.   Roast in the basket of your air fryer toast oven for about 20 minutes, turning the chicken halfway through or until chicken is cooked through.

5.   Serve chicken with kale and almond salad.

Nutrition:

Calories: 293 kcal,

Carbs: 10 g,

Fat: 16.4 g,

Protein: 14 g.

CHAPTER 8:

Meat

24.   Lamb Rack With Lemon Crust

Prep Time: 10 minutes

Cooking Time: 25 minutes

Serving: 5

Ingredients

- 1.7 lbs. frenched rack of lamb

- Salt and black pepper, to taste

- 0.13-lb. dry breadcrumbs

- One teaspoon grated garlic

- 1/2 teaspoon salt

- One teaspoon cumin seeds

- One teaspoon ground cumin

- One teaspoon oil

- ½ teaspoon Grated lemon rind

- One egg, beaten

Directions:

1. Place the lamb rack in a baking tray and pour the whisked egg on top.

2. Whisk the rest of the crusting ingredients in a bowl and spread over the lamb.

3. Press "Power Button" of Air Fry Oven and turn the dial to select the "Air Fry" mode.

4. Press the Time button and again turn the dial to set the cooking time to 25 minutes.

5. Now push the Temp button and rotate the dial to set the temperature at 350 degrees F.

6. Once preheated, place the lamb baking tray in the oven and close its lid.

7. Slice and serve warm.

Nutrition:

Calories 427 Total Fat 5.4 g

Saturated Fat 4.2 g Cholesterol 168 mg

Sodium 203 mg Total Carbs 58.5 g

Sugar 1.1 g Fiber 4 g

Protein 21.9 g

25.   Braised Lamb Shanks

Prep Time: 10 minutes

Cooking Time: 20 minutes

Serving: 4

Ingredients

- Four lamb shanks

- 1½ teaspoons salt

- ½ teaspoon black pepper

- Four garlic cloves, crushed

- Two tablespoons olive oil

- 4 to 6 sprigs fresh rosemary

- 3 cups beef broth, divided

- Two tablespoons balsamic vinegar

Directions:

1.   Place the sham shanks in a baking pan.

2.   Whisk the rest of the ingredients in a bowl and pour over the shanks.

3.   Place these shanks in the Air fryer basket.

4.   Press "Power Button" of Air Fry Oven and turn the dial to select the "Air Fry" mode.

5. Press the Time button and again turn the dial to set the cooking time to 20 minutes.

6. Now push the Temp button and rotate the dial to set the temperature at 360 degrees F.

7. Once preheated, place the Air fryer basket in the oven and close its lid.

8. Slice and serve warm.

Nutrition:

Calories 336

Total Fat 9.7 g

Saturated Fat 4.7 g

Cholesterol 181 mg

Sodium 245 mg

Total Carbs 32.5 g

Fiber 0.3 g

Sugar 1.8 g

Protein 30.3 g

26. Za'atar Lamb Chops

Prep Time: 10 minutes

Cooking Time: 10 minutes

Serving: 8

Ingredients

- Eight lamb loin chops, bone-in

- Three garlic cloves, crushed

- One teaspoon olive oil

- 1/2 fresh lemon

- 1 1/4 teaspoon salt

- One tablespoon Za'atar

- Black pepper, to taste

Directions:

1. Rub the lamb chops with oil, zaatar, salt, lemon juice, garlic, and black pepper.

2. Place these chops in the air fryer basket.

3. Press "Power Button" of Air Fry Oven and turn the dial to select the "Air Fry" mode.

4. Press the Time button and again turn the dial to set the cooking time to 10 minutes.

5. Now push the Temp button and rotate the dial to set the temperature at 400 degrees F.

6. Once preheated, place the air fryer basket in the oven and close its lid.

7. Flip the chops when cooked halfway through, and then resume cooking.

8. Serve warm.

Nutrition:

Calories 391

Total Fat 2.8 g

Saturated Fat 0.6 g

Cholesterol 330 mg

Sodium 62 mg

Total Carbs 36.5 g

Fiber 9.2 g

Sugar 4.5 g

Protein 6.6

27.   Simple Beef Sirloin Roast

Preparation Time: 10 minutes

Cooking Time: 50 minutes

Servings: 8

Ingredients:

- 2½ pounds sirloin roast

- Salt and ground black pepper, as required

Directions:

1.   Rub the roast with salt and black pepper generously.

2.   Insert the rotisserie rod through the roast.

3.   Insert the rotisserie forks, one on each rod's side, to secure the rod to the chicken.

4.   Arrange the drip pan at the bottom of the Instant Vortex plus Air Fryer Oven cooking chamber.

5.   Select "Roast" and then adjust the temperature to 350 degrees F.

6.   Set the timer for 50 minutes and press the "Start."

7.   When the display shows "Add Food," press the red lever down and load the rod's left side into the Vortex.

8.   Now, slide the rod's left side into the groove along the metal bar, so it doesn't move.

9.   Then, close the door and touch "Rotate."

10.   When cooking time is complete, press the red lever to release the rod.

11.   Remove from the Vortex and place the roast onto a platter for about 10 minutes before slicing.

12.   With a sharp knife, cut the roast into desired sized slices and serve.

Nutrition:

Calories 201

Total Fat 8.8 g

Saturated Fat 3.1 g

Cholesterol 94 mg

Sodium 88 mg

Total Carbs 0 g

Fiber 0 g

Sugar 0 g

Protein 28.9 g

28.   Seasoned Beef Roast

Preparation Time: 10 minutes

Cooking Time: 45 minutes

Servings: 10

Ingredients:

- 3 pounds beef top roast

- One tablespoon olive oil

- Two tablespoons Montreal steak seasoning

Directions:

1.   Coat the roast with oil and then rub with the seasoning generously.

2.   With kitchen twines, tie the roast to keep it compact.

3.   Arrange the roast onto the cooking tray.

4.   Arrange the drip pan at the bottom of the Instant Vortex plus Air Fryer Oven cooking chamber.

5.   Select "Air Dry" and then adjust the temperature to 360 degrees F.

6.   Set the timer for 45 minutes and press the "Start."

7.   When the display shows "Add Food," insert the cooking tray in the center position.

8.   When the display shows "Turn Food," do nothing.

9.   When cooking time is complete, remove the tray from Vortex and place the roast onto a platter for about 10 minutes before slicing.

10.   With a sharp knife, cut the roast into desired sized slices and serve.

Nutrition:

Calories 269

Total Fat 9.9 g

Saturated Fat 3.4 g

Cholesterol 122 mg

Sodium 538 mg

Total Carbs 0 g

Fiber 0 g

Sugar 0 g

Protein 41.3 g

29.   Bacon-Wrapped Filet Mignon

Preparation Time: 10 minutes

Cooking Time: 15 minutes

Servings: 2

Ingredients:

- Two bacon slices

- 2 (4-ounce) filet mignon

- Salt and ground black pepper, as required

- Olive oil cooking spray

Directions:

1.   Wrap 1 bacon slice around each filet mignon and secure with toothpicks.

2.   Season the fillets with the salt and black pepper lightly.

3.   Arrange the filet mignon onto a cooling rack and spray with cooking spray.

4.   Arrange the drip pan at the bottom of the Instant Vortex plus Air Fryer Oven cooking chamber.

5.   Select "Air Dry" and then adjust the temperature to 375 degrees F.

6.   Set the timer for 15 minutes and press the "Start."

7.　　　When the display shows "Add Food," insert the cooking rack in the center position.

8.　　　When the display shows "Turn Food," turn the filets.

9.　　　When cooking time is complete, remove the rack from Vortex and serve hot.

Nutrition:

Calories 360

Total Fat 19.6 g

Saturated Fat 6.8 g

Cholesterol 108 mg

Sodium 737 mg

Total Carbs 0.4 g

Fiber 0 g

Sugar 0 g

Protein 42.6 g

30.   Beef Burgers

Preparation 15 minutes Cooking 18 minutes Servings: 4

For Burgers:

- 1 pound ground beef

- ½ cup panko breadcrumbs

- ¼ cup onion, chopped finely

- Three tablespoons Dijon mustard

- Three teaspoons low-sodium soy sauce

- Two teaspoons fresh rosemary, chopped finely

- Salt, to taste

For Topping:

- Two tablespoons Dijon mustard

- One tablespoon brown sugar

- One teaspoon soy sauce

- 4 Gruyere cheese slices

Directions:

1.   In a large bowl, add all the ingredients and mix until well combined.

2.   Make four equal-sized patties from the mixture.

3. Arrange the patties onto a cooking tray.

4. Arrange the drip pan at the bottom of the Instant Vortex plus Air Fryer Oven cooking chamber.

5. Select "Air Dry" and then adjust the temperature to 370 degrees F.

6. Set the timer for 15 minutes and press the "Start."

7. When the display shows "Add Food," insert the cooking rack in the center position.

8. When the display shows "Turn Food," turn the burgers.

9. Meanwhile, for the sauce: In a small bowl, add the mustard, brown sugar, and soy sauce and mix well.

10. When cooking time is complete, remove the tray from Vortex and coat the burgers with the sauce.

11. Top each burger with one cheese slice.

12. Return the tray to the cooking chamber and select "Broil."

13. Set the timer for 3 minutes and press the "Start."

14. When cooking time is complete, remove the tray from Vortex and serve hot.

Nutrition: Calories 402 Total Fat 18 g Saturated Fat 8.5 g Cholesterol 133mg Sodium 651 mg Total Carbs 6.3 g Fiber 0.8 g

Sugar 3 g Protein 44.4 g

CHAPTER 9:

Vegetables

31.   Blistered Shishito Peppers

Preparation Time: 10minutes

Cooking Time: 6 minutes

Serving: 4

Ingredients:

Dipping Sauce:

- 1 cup sour cream

- Two tablespoons fresh lemon juice

- One clove garlic, minced

- One green onion (white and green parts), finely chopped

- Peppers:

- 8 ounces (227 g) shishito peppers

- One tablespoon vegetable oil

- One teaspoon toasted sesame oil

- Kosher salt and black pepper, to taste

- ¼ to ½ teaspoon red pepper flakes

- ½ teaspoon toasted sesame seeds

Directions:

1. In a small bowl, stir all the ingredients for the dipping sauce to combine. Cover and refrigerate until serving time.

2. Press Start/Cancel. Preheat the air fryer oven to 400°F (204°C).

3. Toss the peppers with the vegetable oil. Then put the peppers in the fry basket.

4. Insert the fry basket at mid position. Select Air Fry, Convection, and set time to 6 minutes or until peppers are lightly charred in spots, stirring the peppers halfway through the cooking time.

5. Transfer the peppers to a serving bowl.

6. Drizzle with the sesame oil and toss to coat—season with salt and pepper.

7. Sprinkle with the red pepper and sesame seeds and toss again.

8. Serve immediately with the dipping sauce.

32.   Mascarpone Mushrooms

Preparation Time: 10minutes

Cooking Time: 15 minutes

Serving: 4

Ingredients:

- Vegetable oil spray

- 4 cups sliced mushrooms

- One medium yellow onion, chopped

- Two cloves garlic, minced

- ¼ cup heavy whipping cream or half-and-half

- 8 ounces (227 g) mascarpone cheese

- One teaspoon dried thyme

- One teaspoon kosher salt

- One teaspoon black pepper

- ½ teaspoon red pepper flakes

- 4 cups cooked konjac noodles, for serving

- ½ cup grated Parmesan cheese

Directions:

1. Press Start/Cancel. Preheat the air fryer oven to 350°F (177°C). Spray a heatproof pan with vegetable oil spray.

2. In a medium bowl, combine the mushrooms, onion, garlic, cream, mascarpone, thyme, salt, black pepper, and red pepper flakes. Stir to combine. Transfer the mixture to the prepared pan.

3. Put the pan in the fry basket. Insert at a low position. Select Bake, Convection, and set time to 15 minutes, stirring halfway through the baking time.

4. Divide the pasta among four shallow bowls. Spoon the mushroom mixture evenly over the pasta. Sprinkle with Parmesan cheese and serve.

Vegetable Sides

33.   Air Fried Asparagus

Preparation Time: 5minutes

Cooking Time: 5 minutes

Serving: 4

Ingredients:

- 1 pound (454 g) fresh asparagus spears, trimmed

- One tablespoon olive oil

- Salt and ground black pepper, to taste

Directions:

1.   Press Start/Cancel. Preheat the air fryer oven to 375°F (191°C).

2.   Combine all the ingredients and transfer them to the fry basket. Insert the fry basket at mid position.

3.   Select Air Fry, Convection, and set time to 5 minutes, or until soft.

4.   Serve hot.

34.   Cheesy Macaroni Balls

Preparation Time: 10minutes

Cooking Time: 10 minutes

Serving: 2

Ingredients:

- 2 cups leftover macaroni

- 1 cup shredded Cheddar cheese

- ½ cup flour

- 1 cup bread crumbs

- Three large eggs

- 1 cup milk

- ½ teaspoon salt

- ¼ teaspoon black pepper

Directions:

1.   Press Start/Cancel. Preheat the air fryer oven to 365°F (185°C).

2.   In a bowl, combine the leftover macaroni and shredded cheese.

3.   Pour the flour into a separate bowl. Put the bread crumbs in a third bowl. Finally, in a fourth bowl, mix the eggs and milk with a whisk.

4.   With an ice-cream scoop, create balls from the macaroni mixture. Coat them the flour, then in the egg mixture, and lastly in the bread crumbs.

5.   Arrange the balls in the fry basket and insert the fry basket at mid position. Select Air Fry, Convection, and set time to 10 minutes, giving them an occasional stir. Ensure they crisp up nicely.

6.   Serve hot.

35.   Crispy Chickpeas

Preparation Time: 5minutes

Cooking Time: 15 minutes

Serving: 4

Ingredients:

- 1 (15-ounces / 425-g) canned chickpeas, drained but not rinsed

- Two tablespoons olive oil

- One teaspoon salt

- Two tablespoons lemon juice

Directions:

1.   Press Start/Cancel. Preheat the air fryer oven to 400°F (204°C).

2.   Combine all the ingredients into a bowl. Then transfer this to the fry basket. Insert the fry basket at mid position.

3.   Select Air Fry, Convection, and set time to 15 minutes, ensuring the chickpeas become nice and crispy.

4.   Serve immediately.

CHAPTER 10:

Soup

36.   Broccoli And Chicken Soup

Preparation Time: 35 minutes

Cooking Time: 30 minutes

Servings: 4

Ingredients:

- Four boneless chicken thighs, diced

- One small carrot, chopped

- One broccoli head, broken into florets

- One garlic clove, chopped

- One small onion, chopped

- 4 cups of water

- 3 tbsp. extra virgin olive oil

- 1/2 tsp. salt, black pepper, to taste

Directions:

1. In a deep soup pot, heat olive oil and gently sauté broccoli for 2-3 minutes, stirring occasionally. Add in onion, carrot, chicken, and cook, stirring, for 2-3 minutes.

2. Stir in salt, black pepper, and water. Bring to a boil.

Simmer for 30 minutes, then remove from heat and set aside to cool. In a blender or food processor, blend soup until completely smooth. Serve and enjoy

CHAPTER 11:

Snacks

37. Potato Nuggets

Preparation Time: 10 minutes

Cooking Time: 42 minutes

Serve: 4

Ingredients:

- 2 cups potatoes, chopped

- One garlic clove, minced

- 1 tsp. olive oil

- 2 tbsp. almond milk

- 4 cups kale, chopped

- Pepper

- Salt

Directions:

1. Insert wire rack in rack position 4. Select air fry, set temperature 390 F, timer for 12 minutes. Press start to preheat the oven.

2. Add potatoes in boiling water and cook for 30 minutes or until tender. Drain well.

3. Heat oil in a pan over medium-high heat.

4. Add garlic and sauté for 30 seconds. Add kale and sauté for 2 minutes.

5. Transfer sautéed garlic and kale in a large bowl. Add potatoes, almond milk, pepper, salt, and mash potato using a fork and stir to combine.

6. Make small nuggets from potato mixture and place on an air fryer basket, and air fry for 12 minutes.

7. Serve and enjoy.

Nutrition:

Calories 113

Fat 3 g

Carbohydrates 19.5 g

Sugar 1.1 g

38.   Tasty Zucchini Patties

Preparation Time: 10 minutes

Cooking Time: 25 minutes

Serve: 6

Ingredients:

- 1 cup zucchini, shredded and squeeze out all liquid

- 2 tbsp. onion, minced

- One egg, lightly beaten

- 1/4 tsp. red pepper flakes

- 1/4 cup parmesan cheese, grated

- 1/2 tbsp. Dijon mustard

- 1/2 tbsp. mayonnaise

- 1/2 cup breadcrumbs

- Pepper

- Salt

Directions:

1.   Insert wire rack in rack position 4. Select air fry, set temperature 400 F, timer for 25 minutes. Press start to preheat the oven.

2. Add all ingredients into the bowl and mix until well combined.

3. Make small patties from the zucchini mixture, place it on an air fryer basket, and air fry for 25 minutes.

4. Serve and enjoy.

Nutrition:

Calories 68

Fat 2.5 g

Carbohydrates 8 g

Sugar 1.2 g

Protein 3.7 g

Cholesterol 30 mg

39.   Beef Enchilada Dip

Preparation Time: 5 minutes

Cooking time: 10 minutes

Servings: 8

Ingredients:

- 2 lbs. ground beef

- ½ onion, chopped fine

- Two cloves garlic, chopped fine

- 2 cups enchilada sauce

- 2 cups Monterrey Jack cheese, grated

- 2 tbsp. sour cream

Directions:

1. Place rack in position 1.

2. Heat a large skillet over med-high heat. Add beef and cook until it starts to brown. Drain off fat.

3. Stir in onion and garlic and cook until tender, about 3 minutes. Stir in enchilada sauce and transfer mixture to a small casserole dish and top with cheese.

4.   Set oven to convection bake at 325°F for 10 minutes. After 5 minutes, add casserole to the range and bake 3-5 minutes until cheese is melted and the mixture is heated through.

5.   Serve warm topped with sour cream.

Nutrition:

Calories 414, Total Fat 22g, Saturated Fat 10g, Total Carbs 15g, Net Carbs 11g, Protein 39g, Sugar 8g, Fiber 4g, Sodium 1155mg, Potassium 635mg, Phosphorus 385mg

40.   Meatballs In Thermo Mix And Air Fryer

Preparation Time: 10 minutes

Cooking time: 35 minutes

Servings: 6

Ingredients

- 1 kg mixed minced meat

- One onion

- One egg

- One bunch of parsley

- Two cloves of garlic

- One lemon

- Salt

- Ground pepper

- Bread crumbs

- Extra virgin olive oil

Directions:

1.   We put the minced meat in a bowl.

2.   Salpimentamos.

3. In the Thermomix glass, we put the onion cut into quarters, the egg, the parsley, the garlic, and the lemon juice.

4. We select 7 seconds speed 5.

5. We dump the content in the minced meat and bind.

6. Add some breadcrumbs so that the meat loses some moisture.

7. We make the meatballs and go through the breadcrumbs.

8. Put the meatballs in batches in the basket of the air fryer and close the drawer.

9. We spray with oil.

10. We select 10 minutes of 200 degrees. We shake the basket and leave three more minutes.

11. We take out and make another batch of meatballs.

12. We serve

41.   Fried Sardines In The Air Fryer

Preparation Time: 10 minutes

Cooking time: 30 minutes

Servings: 6

Ingredients

- 12 sardines

- Fishmeal

- Salt

- Extra virgin olive oil

Directions:

1. We clean the sardines, remove guts, and, if we want, the heads.

2. We put salt.

3. We pass the sardines for flour and shake well to remove the excess flour.

4. We put sardines, 4 in 4 or 6 in 6, in the air fryer basket, depending on the size, do not pile up.

5. We spray with oil.

6. We close the drawer with the basket inside.

7. We select between 180 to 200. Cook for about 10 minutes. Set a high temperature to make sardines crispy and golden.

8. At 10 minutes, we shake the sardines and check if they are ready or need a few more minutes.

9. When they are golden brown to our liking, we take out. We serve

10. Remember that there are no foods with the same color in this type of fryers when we fry the food submerged in oil.

CHAPTER 12:

Desserts

42. Cherry Pancakes

Preparation Time: 10 minutes

Cooking Time: 25 minutes

Serving: 4

Ingredients

- 2TB. Cherries torn to bits

- 1 1/2 tablespoon almond flour

- Four Eggs

- 2Tps. Clean basil

- 2Tps. Dry peters

- Pepper and salt to taste

- Three tbs. Butter-Butter

Directions:

1.   The air fryer is preheated to 250 Fahrenheit.

2.   Mix the ingredients in a tiny bowl. Ensure the mix is smooth and well balanced.

3.   Take a mold from a pancake and grind it with butter. Attach the batter to the mold and place it in the bowl of the air-fryer.

4.   Cook until all sides of the pancake are browned; serve with maple syrup.

43.   Apple Fritters

Preparation Time: 4 minutes

Cooking Time: 5 minutes

Serving: 15

Ingredients:

- Fritters

- 14 oz. raspberries

- ½ cup of confectioner's sugar

- 1tablespoon of cinnamon

- 1large apple peeled and chopped

- 1cup of self-rising flour

- 1cup of plain Greek yogurt

- 2teaspoons of sugar

- Glaze

- 1cup of confectioner's sugar

- 2tablespoons of milk or more, if needed

Directions:

1.   Set the Instant Vortex on an Air fryer to 370 degrees F for 15 minutes. Combine all the ingredients for patties in a bowl to form a smooth dough. Whip sugar with milk to

form a glaze. Divide the fritter dough into four portions and place it on the cooking tray. Press the fritter balls to flatten slightly.

2.   Insert the cooking tray in the Vortex when it displays "Add Food." Flip the sides when it shows "Turn Food." Remove from the oven when cooking time is complete. Serve topped with glaze.

Nutrition:

Calories: 248   Protein: 14.1gCarbs: 31.4gFat: 15.7g

44.   Peanut Butter Banana Bites

Preparation Time: 5minutes

Cooking Time: 6 minutes

Serving: 5

Ingredients:

- 6wonton wrappers

- 1/2 cup of peanut butter

- 2teaspoons of vegetable oil

- 1large banana, sliced

Directions:

1. Set the Instant Vortex on an Air fryer to 380 degrees F for 6 minutes. Arrange one teaspoon of peanut butter and one banana slice in the middle of each wonton wrapper. Drench the wrapper edges with water and seal the opposite sides.

2. Place the wrappers on the cooking tray and drizzle with oil. Insert the cooking tray in the Vortex when it displays "Add Food." Flip the sides when it shows "Turn Food." Remove from the oven when cooking time is complete. Serve warm.

Nutrition: Calories: 253   Protein: 8.8gCarbs: 27.9gFat: 12.9g

45.   Healthy Apple Crisp

Preparation Time: 5 minutes

Cooking Time: 20 minutes

Serving: 4

Ingredients:

- 1/3 cup of quick oats

- 1/4 cup of brown sugar

- 2tablespoons of light butter melted

- 1/2 teaspoon of cinnamon

- 3cups of apples chopped

- 1tablespoon of pure maple syrup

- 2teaspoons of lemon juice

- 3tablespoons of almond flour

Directions:

1.   Set the Instant Vortex on an Air fryer to 350 degrees F for 20 minutes. Combine apples with lemon juice, one tablespoon almond flour, cinnamon, and maple syrup in a bowl. Mingle oats, melted butter, brown sugar, and remaining almond flour in another bowl. Pour the oats mixture into the apple mixture.

2.   Transfer this mixture to the cooking tray. Insert the cooking tray in the Vortex when it displays "Add Food." Flip the sides when it shows "Turn Food." Remove from the oven when cooking time is complete. Serve warm.

Nutrition:

Calories: 213   Protein: 12gCarbs: 55gFat: 14g

46.   Cranberry Scones

Preparation Time: 5 minutes

Cooking Time: 10 minutes

Serving: 4

Ingredients:

- 1cup of fresh cranberries

- ⅓ cup of sugar

- 1tablespoon of orange zest

- ¾ cup of half and half cream

- 2cups of flour

- ¼ teaspoon of ground nutmeg

- ¼ teaspoon of salt

- ¼ cup of butter, chilled and diced

- ¼ cup of brown sugar

- 1tablespoon of baking powder

- 1egg

Directions:

1.   Set the Instant Vortex on an Air fryer to 365 degrees F for 10 minutes: strain nutmeg, flour, baking powder, salt, and sugar in a bowl.

2.   Blend in the cream and egg. Fold in the orange zest and cranberries to form a smooth dough.

3.   Roll the dough and cut into scones. Place the scones on the cooking tray. Insert the cooking tray in the Vortex when it displays "Add Food." Flip the sides when it shows "Turn Food." Remove from the oven when cooking time is complete. Serve warm.

Nutrition:

Calories: 219   Protein: 5.2gCarbs: 23.7gFat: 19.7g

47.   Blueberry Apple Crumble

Preparation Time: 5 minutes

Cooking Time: 15 minutes

Serving: 6

Ingredients:

- 1medium apple, finely diced

- 1/2 cup of frozen blueberries strawberries

- 2/3 cup of rice flour

- 2tablespoons of sugar

- 1/2 teaspoon of ground cinnamon

- 2tablespoons of non-dairy butter

Directions:

1.   Set the Instant Vortex on an Air fryer to 350 degrees F for 15 minutes.

2.   Combine apple with blueberries in a bowl.

3.   Mingle butter with flour, cinnamon, and sugar in another bowl.

4.   Pour the butter mixture into the apple mixture.

5. Transfer this mixture to the cooking tray. Insert the cooking tray in the Vortex when it displays "Add Food." Flip the sides when it shows "Turn Food."

6. Remove from the oven when cooking time is complete. Serve warm.

Nutrition:

Calories: 379   Protein: 5.2gCarbs: 23.7gFat: 29.7g

48. Air Fried Apple Pie

Preparation Time: 5minutes

Cooking Time: 30 minutes

Serving: 6

Ingredients:

- 1large apple, chopped

- 2teaspoons of lemon juice

- 1tablespoon of ground cinnamon

- 1pie crust, refrigerated

- Baking spray

- ½ teaspoon of vanilla extract

- 1tablespoon of butter

- 1beaten egg

- 1tablespoon of raw sugar

- 2tablespoons of sugar

Directions:

1. Set the Instant Vortex on an Air fryer to 350 degrees F for 30 minutes. Split the pie crust into two halves and spread into an 8-inch greased pan. Combine apple with sugar, cinnamon, lemon juice, and vanilla extract in a bowl

2.   Empty the apple mixture into the pie crust and cover with the pie crust half.

3.   Seal the edges and brush the whisked egg on the top.

4.   Sprinkle the pie with raw sugar and place it on the cooking tray.

5.   Insert the cooking tray in the Vortex when it displays "Add Food." Flip the sides when it shows "Turn Food." Remove from the oven when cooking time is complete. Serve warm.

Nutrition

Calories: 368   Protein: 7.2gCarbs: 72.8gFat: 6g

49.   Air Fryer Biscuit Donuts

Preparation Time: 5 minutes Cooking Time: 5 minutes

Serving: 4

Ingredients:

- Coconut oil

- 1can of biscuit dough, pre-made

- 1/2 cup of white sugar

- 1/2 cup of powdered sugar

- 2tablespoons of melted butter

- 2teaspoons of cinnamon

Directions:

1.   Set the Instant Vortex on an Air fryer to 350 degrees F for 5 minutes. Cut the dough with the biscuit cutter. Brush the coconut oil on the cooking tray and place the biscuits on it. Insert the cooking tray in the Vortex when it displays "Add Food." Flip the sides when it shows "Turn Food."

2.   Remove from the oven when cooking time is complete. Drizzle the melted butter over the donuts and coat with either the cinnamon-sugar mixture or the powdered sugar.

Nutrition:

Calories: 301   Protein: 8.8gCarbs: 25gFat: 32.2g

CHAPTER 13:

Special Recipe

50.   Sweet Baby Carrots Dish

Preparation Time: 10 minutes

Cooking Time: 10 Minutes

Servings: 4

Ingredients

- 2 cups baby carrots
- A pinch of salt and black pepper
- 1 tbsp. brown sugar
- ½ tbsp. butter

Directions

1. Blend baby carrots with butter, pepper, salt and sugar in a bowl, toss, put into air fryer and cook at 350° F for 10 minutes.
2. Share in plates.
3. Serve.

Nutrition:

Calories: 76 kcal

Protein: 1.09 g

Fat: 5.87 g

Carbohydrates: 5.91 g

Conclusion

If you are a fan of smart cooking, then Air Fryer Toaster Oven Cookbook is a perfect fit for you. With this new kitchen miracle, you don't need to switch from appliance to appliance to get various delicious meals., you can roast, toast, Air fry, bake, and cook much more. If you haven't brought this kitchen bliss to home or you have it but haven't been able to use it to its full potential, then this cookbook is a right pick! Now you can toast fresh bread slices in the morning and bake an irresistible chicken for dinner, all just by using Air Fryer Toaster Oven.

CPSIA information can be obtained
at www.ICGtesting.com
Printed in the USA
BVHW091125230221
600894BV00003B/443